A New True Book

OSTRICHES

By Emilie U. Lepthien

CHILDRENS PRESS®
CHICAGO

Ostrich chick

PHOTO CREDITS

© Reinhard Brucker—11, 27

H. Armstrong Roberts—© David Lorenz Winston, 18, 23; © Camerique, 42

Emilie Lepthien—37 (left), 41 (left), 43

Photri—25, 32, 35

© Carl Purcell—8, 17

Root Resources—© Charles G. Summers, Jr., 29, 30

© James P. Rowan—44

Tom Stack & Associates—© Buff Corsi, 7 (right); © Barbara von Hoffmann, 16; © Charles G. Summers, Jr., 28

© Lynn M. Stone—2, 6 (left), 7 (left), 31, 37 (right), 41 (right), 45

SuperStock International, Inc.—© A. Kaiser, Cover; © M. Bruce, 33

Tony Stone Images—© Brian Seed, 4; © Nicholas DeVore, 13; © Chris Harvey, 24

Valan—© Pam E. Hickman, 14

Visuals Unlimited—© Charles Rushing, Cover Inset; © John D. Cunningham, 6 (right), 15; © D. Long, 9; © Will Troyer, 12; © Walt Anderson, 20; © Steve McCutcheon, 39

Cover: Ostriches, Masai Mara, Kenya

Cover Inset: Close-up of ostrich head

Project Editor: Fran Dyra
Design: Margrit Fiddle

Library of Congress Cataloging-in-Publication Data

Lepthien, Emilie U. (Emilie Utteg)
    Ostriches / by Emilie U. Lepthien.
        p.   cm. — (A New true book)
    Includes index.
    Summary: Describes the physical characteristics, behavior, and life cycle of this large flightless bird.
    ISBN 0-516-01193-6
    1. Ostriches—Juvenile literature.
[1. Ostriches.] I. Title.
QL696.S9L47   1993
598.5'1—dc20   93-3407
                                  CIP
                                  AC

TABLE OF CONTENTS

Birds on an ostrich
farm in South Africa

WHAT IS AN OSTRICH?

Ostriches are the biggest birds in the world. They live on the deserts and plains of Africa. Ostriches belong to a group of birds called ratites.

The rhea (left) has larger wings and more head and neck feathers than an ostrich. The cassowary (above) has a bony growth on its head.

Ratites include the ostrich, the rhea of South America, the cassowary and the emu of Australia, and the kiwi of New Zealand.

Ratites cannot fly. They

The emu (left) has tiny wings and thick, dark brown feathers. The kiwi (right) has a long, slender beak. It is the smallest ratite.

are large, running birds with flat breastbones and small wings. They do not have the heavy muscles attached to the breastbone that enable other birds to fly.

An ostrich's neck makes up almost half its height.

Ostriches have very long legs. The adult male stands about 8 feet (2.4 meters) tall. Their slender neck is at least 3 feet (1 meter) long.

The
female ostrich
(far left) is
smaller than
the male (left).

Male birds may weigh
as much as 300 pounds
(135 kilograms). Female
ostriches, or hens, are
somewhat smaller.

Ostriches can live to

9

be 80 years old. They
mate until they are 40 to
45 years old.

People used to believe
the ostrich buried its small
head in the sand, thinking
no one could see it. But
that isn't true. Actually, the
male is using his beak to
scrape out a hole in which
the hens will lay their eggs.

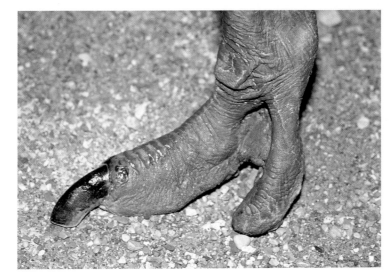

Close-up of
the ostrich's
unusual toes.

TOES, FEET, AND LEGS

Ostriches have only two toes on each foot. One is a small toe that helps the bird keep its balance. The other toe is very large, and its toenail is strong enough to rip open a lion's belly.

Ostriches can also deliver a powerful forward

kick. One kick from an ostrich can break a hyena's back. It is wise to stay out of the way of an angry ostrich.

What you might think are an ostrich's knees are really its ankles. Its knees are close to its hips.

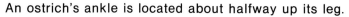
An ostrich's ankle is located about halfway up its leg.

Ostriches walk like camels.

Ancient people called
ostriches "camel birds"
because they have a
humping walk like a
camel. From a distance, in
the desert sands of Africa,
they might easily be
mistaken for a camel.   **13**

The beautiful black feathers and white plumes of the male ostrich are used to decorate clothes.

WINGS AND FEATHERS

Adult male ostriches have black feathers on their body. They have long white feathers called plumes on their tail and

The male ostrich has showy plumes, but the female's feathers are dull grayish-brown.

wings. Their legs and neck have almost no feathers. The hens' feathers are gray-brown.

When ostriches run, they use their wings to help lift them off the ground. With this "lift" and their very

15

Ostriches are found in open country where there are few places to hide. But their great speed enables them to outrun most predators.

long legs, they can take strides of 25 feet (7.6 meters). They can run at speeds of up to 40 miles (64 kilometers) per hour. An ostrich can outrun a horse.

Ostriches are handsome, graceful birds when they run. On ostrich farms in South Africa they often compete in races. Sometimes they are trained to pull small carts or carry riders on their backs.

Ostriches carrying riders in South Africa

Without teeth or a tongue, ostriches must swallow their food whole.

FOOD AND EATING

Ostriches have no teeth. They have no tongue, either. In the wild, they live on grasses, seeds, fruits, and leaves. They also eat small animals—such as lizards, frogs, birds, and worms.

On ostrich farms, the birds are fed a special diet of prepared food and minerals.

Ostriches can go for long periods without water, but they drink it whenever they can. They also get water from their food. And they like to take a bath and go for a swim.

The ostrich has a jaw that slides sideways. This helps the bird to swallow.

Ostriches get much of the water they need from their food, but they also drink when they can find a water hole.

Ostriches have two stomachs. Since they have no teeth, they cannot chew their food. Instead, they swallow coarse sand and small stones. The stones help to grind up their food.

Sometimes ostriches swallow nails and other metal objects—even aluminum cans. The owners of ostrich farms must pick up any metal lying on the ground. Often they use metal detectors. If they think a bird has swallowed a dangerous metal object, they X-ray the bird's body. Sometimes, an operation is needed to remove the metal.

SPECIAL ADAPTATIONS

A soft down covers the ostrich's neck. The skin on the neck may be red, blue, or black. There are no feathers on the head.

Ostriches have large eyes with beautiful long lashes. They have very keen eyesight. In some African countries, they graze with herds of zebras and antelope. Their long necks and excellent eyesight allow ostriches to see danger a long way off. Then they warn the animals nearby.

Ostriches have no vocal chords. However, their hissing and roaring sounds can be heard far away.

A male ostrich bows to a hen during the mating dance.

MATING, NESTING, AND EGGS

When the males are ready to mate, the skin on their shins and beaks turns red. The males spin around and do a mating dance. The hens shake their feathers.

In the wild, male ostriches usually mate with two to seven hens. The male scrapes out a hole in the ground for a nest. The nest is about 2 feet (0.6 meter) deep and 5 feet (1.5 meters) across.

All of the male's hens lay their eggs in the same nest. There may be from 15 to 60 eggs in each nest.

The nest is a shallow pit dug in sandy soil.

When the female is ready to lay an egg, she leans forward and spreads out her wings. Each hen lays from 6 to 14 eggs, one every other day during the mating period. In one year, a hen may lay 40 to 80 eggs.

The average egg is about 6 inches (15 centimeters) long and 5 inches (13 centimeters) wide. Ostrich eggs are the largest eggs of any living bird. One ostrich egg

An ostrich egg is about six inches long.

equals about two dozen chicken's eggs. It weighs between 3 and 3½ pounds (1.3 and 1.5 kilograms). The eggshells are very smooth and hard.

The male ostrich sits on the eggs from late in the afternoon until early morning. Keeping the eggs warm in this way is called

Male ostrich preparing to sit on its eggs

Female ostrich sitting on the nest

incubating. Sometimes a
hen sits on the eggs
during the day. The eggs
hatch after about 42 days.

In the wild, in places
where the climate is warm,
it may not be necessary
to incubate the eggs
throughout the entire day.

29

A male ostrich pretends to have a broken wing in order to lead an enemy away from its chicks.

If the eggs or young birds are in danger, the male and females protect them. They pretend to be injured and lead the predator away from the nest.

On ostrich farms, the

Ostrich eggs in
an incubator

eggs are kept in
incubators. The eggs are
turned every hour.

Before the eggs hatch,
they are candled—held in
front of a bright light. This
is done to make sure
each egg has an air
pocket at the top. The
pocket holds enough air to
keep the chick alive for 30

An ostrich watches over the hatching chicks.
Many eggs fail to hatch.

hours. It takes this long
for the chick to break
through the hard shell.
Sometimes the chick
needs human help.

CHICKS GROW UP

Ostrich chicks are almost as big as a chicken when they hatch. They weigh about 2½ pounds (1 kilogram) and stand 9 to 12 inches (23 to 30 centimeters) tall.

They have rough

body feathers. The neck and head are covered with spotted down—fluffy, fine feathers. The neck and head feathers disappear as the chicks grow older.

A chick can walk soon after it hatches. When it is only a month old, it can run as fast as an adult.

Young ostriches grow about 12 inches (30 centimeters) each month. They are called juveniles when they are a year old.

Street salesman selling wild ostrich feathers

PROFITS AND PLUMES

For two thousand years, ostrich plumes have been used as decorations. Over the centuries, so many birds were killed for their feathers that the ostrich could have become extinct. But ostrich plumes went out of style. When there was no money to be made, the birds were not hunted as much. Ostrich farmers in South Africa destroyed 200,000 birds.

But there are still many uses for ostrich feathers. They make beautiful coats and jackets. They are also used to decorate clothing. And they make fine feather dusters.

Every six to seven

White ostrich-plume jackets (left), and feather dusters
(right) made from dyed ostrich feathers

months, the farmer cuts off
plumes from the underside
of a bird's wings. This
does not hurt the ostrich.
The stumps of the feathers
fall out, and new feathers
begin to grow.

Today, the soft, durable ostrich hide is used to make purses, briefcases, boots, and other leather items.

Ostrich meat tastes like beef but has less fat than beef or chicken. The meat may become a popular food in the future.

Birds on an ostrich farm in South Africa

OSTRICH FARMS

There are about 1,200 ostrich farms in the United States. They are found mainly in the southern and western states: Florida, Texas, Arizona, Oklahoma, southern California, and the Carolinas.

Ostriches are valuable. A breeding pair costs up to $30,000. A three-month-old chick is worth $2,500 and increases $500 in value each month.

On ostrich farms, as soon as a chick is hatched, a microchip is inserted in the back of its neck. The bird's birth date and other important facts are recorded on the microchip. This helps to

An ostrich farmer (left) checks six-week-old ostrich chicks.
A young male ostrich (right) greets visitors at an ostrich
farm in California.

identify the bird throughout
its lifetime.

Ostrich farming is
becoming an important
business. To encourage
farmers to raise ostriches,
some states do not charge
sales tax on ostrich feed.

41

A CURIOUS BIG BIRD

Signs warn visitors to an ostrich farm about the birds' tricks.

No bird is more curious or nosy than an ostrich. It will nip at anything shiny. Unsuspecting visitors may lose their eyeglasses, watches, or keys—even their buttons.

Two organizations of ostrich farmers, Ostrich Farms of North America and the American Ostrich Association, provide members with information about the raising, breeding, health, and marketing of ostriches.

Hand-painted
ostrich eggs
for sale as
decorations

Some scientists think
that ostriches descended
from dinosaurs that
roamed the Earth millions
of years ago. So when
you look at an ostrich, not
only are you seeing the
biggest bird alive today—
you might even be seeing
a descendant of a dinosaur!

45

WORDS YOU SHOULD KNOW

ancient (AIN • shent) — very old; living long ago

antelope (AN • tih • lohp) — a very fast animal that looks like a deer

breastbone (BREST • bone) — the bone at the front of the chest, to which the ribs are attached

camel (KAM • il) — a large animal with a humped back

cassowary (KASS • eh • wer • ee) — a large, flightless bird with a bony growth like a helmet on its head and brownish-black, bristlelike feathers on its body

climate (KLY • mit) — the average kind of weather at a certain place

curious (KYOO • ree • us) — eager to explore and learn things

down (DOWN) — soft, fluffy feathers

durable (DOO • rah • bil) — lasting a long time; not wearing out easily

emu (E • myoo) — a large bird related to but smaller than the ostrich

extinct (ex • TINKT) — no longer living

graceful (GRAIS • ful) — having beauty of form or movement

hide (HYDE) — the skin

incubate (ING • kyoo • bait) — to keep warm

juveniles (JOO • vuh • nyles) — young animals

kiwi (KEE • wee) — a small flightless bird of New Zealand

metal detector (MEH • til dih • TEK • ter) — a device that helps people find metal objects

microchip (MY • kroh • chip) — a tiny piece of material such as silicon on which information can be recorded electronically

mineral (MIN • er • il) — a substance such as iron or calcium that is needed by the body in small amounts

organization (or • guh • nih • ZAY • shun) — a group of people who get together for some special purpose

plumes (PLOOMZ) — big, fluffy feathers

predator (PREH •duh •ter) — an animal that hunts other animals for food

ratite (RAT •ite) — any of a number of large running birds with small wings and a flat breastbone

rhea (REE •uh) — a large flightless bird of South America

stride (STRYDE) — a step

vocal chords (VOH •kil KORDZ) — organs in the neck that make sounds when air is breathed across them

X-ray (X RAY) — to take a picture using rays that show the inside of the body

zebra (ZEE •bruh) — a striped animal that looks like a small horse

INDEX

About the Author

Emilie U. Lepthien received her BA and MS degrees and certificate in school administration from Northwestern University. She taught upper-grade science and social studies, wrote and narrated science programs for the Chicago Public Schools' station WBEZ, and was principal in Chicago, Illinois, for twenty years. She received the American Educator's Medal from Freedoms Foundation.

She is a member of Delta Kappa Gamma Society International, Chicago Principals' Association, Illinois Women's Press Association, National Federation of Press Women, and AAUW.

She has written books in the Enchantment of the World, New True Books, and America the Beautiful series.